As Good As Gold

By Carol M. Elliott

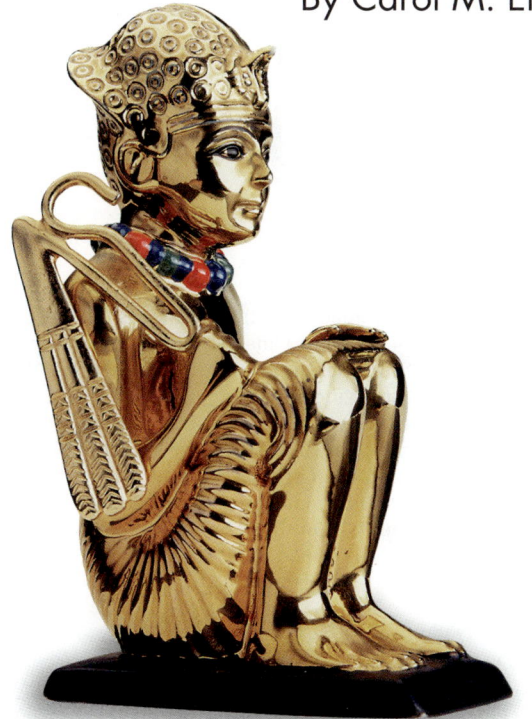

Scott Foresman
is an imprint of

PEARSON

Glenview, Illinois • Boston, Massachusetts • Chandler, Arizona • Upper Saddle River, New Jersey

Photographs

Every effort has been made to secure permission and provide appropriate credit for photographic material. The publisher deeply regrets any omission and pledges to correct errors called to its attention in subsequent editions.

Unless otherwise acknowledged, all photographs are the property of Pearson Education, Inc.

Photo locators denoted as follows: Top (T), Center (C), Bottom (B), Left (L), Right (R), Background (Bkgd)

Opener: ©Andy Sotiriou/Getty Images; **3** (R) ©DK Images, (C) ©Paul Wilkinson/©DK Images, (L) Jupiter Images; **4** (C) Jupiter Images, (TL) ©Patrick Lynch/Alamy Images; **5** (CR) ©Paul Wilkinson/©DK Images, (L) ©Andrew Ammendolia/Alamy Images, (TR) Jupiter Images; **6** (Inset) ©Dave King/©DK Images, (Bkgd) ©Steven Heald/Alamy Images; **7** (TL) Alamy Images, (TR) Hoberman Collection/Corbis, (CR) ©Paul Almasy/Corbis; **8** (T) Jupiter Images; **9** ©Sam Diephuls/Getty Images; **10** ©Andy Sotiriou/Getty Images; **11** ©How Hwee Young/epa/Corbis; **12** ©Blend Images/SuperStock; **13** ©Horizon International Images Limited/Alamy Images; **14** ©Don Johnston/Stone/Getty Images; **15** ©Radius Images/Alamy; **16** (TC) ©Andy Sotiriou/Getty Images, (TL, CL) ©Sam Diephuls/Getty Images, (TR) Alamy Images, (C) ©Dave King/©DK Images, (BR) Jupiter Images.

ISBN 13: 978-0-328-47295-6
ISBN 10:   0-328-47295-6

Copyright © by Pearson Education, Inc., or its affiliates. All rights reserved. Printed in the United States of America. This publication is protected by copyright, and permission should be obtained from the publisher prior to any prohibited reproduction, storage in a retrieval system, or transmission in any form or by any means, electronic, mechanical, photocopying, recording, or likewise. For information regarding permissions, write to Pearson Curriculum Rights & Permissions, One Lake Street, Upper Saddle River, New Jersey 07458.

Pearson® is a trademark, in the U.S. and/or in other countries, of Pearson plc or its affiliates.
Scott Foresman® is a trademark, in the U.S. and/or in other countries, of Pearson Education, Inc., or its affiliates.

3 4 5 6 7 8 9 10 V010 13 12 11 10

Table of Contents

Good as Gold!... 4
Qualities of Gold 6
Gold in Electronics...................................... 8
Gold Keeps Out Heat 12
Gold Keeps Us Safe..................................14

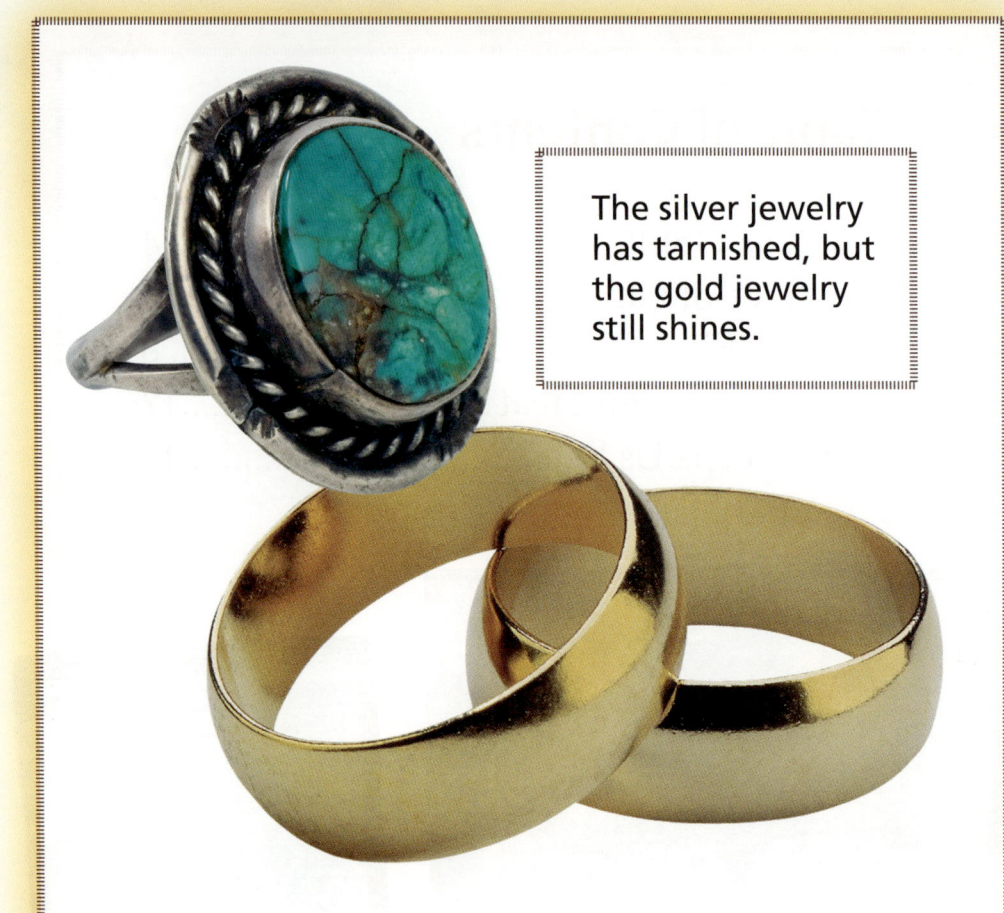

The silver jewelry has tarnished, but the gold jewelry still shines.

Good as Gold!

Gold always shines. It doesn't get dull or change as other metals do. If you look at old jewelry, the silver jewelry might look black, or tarnished, but gold jewelry will still be shiny.

Gold Mined in One Year

- Jewelry
- Coins and Bars
- Industrial Uses

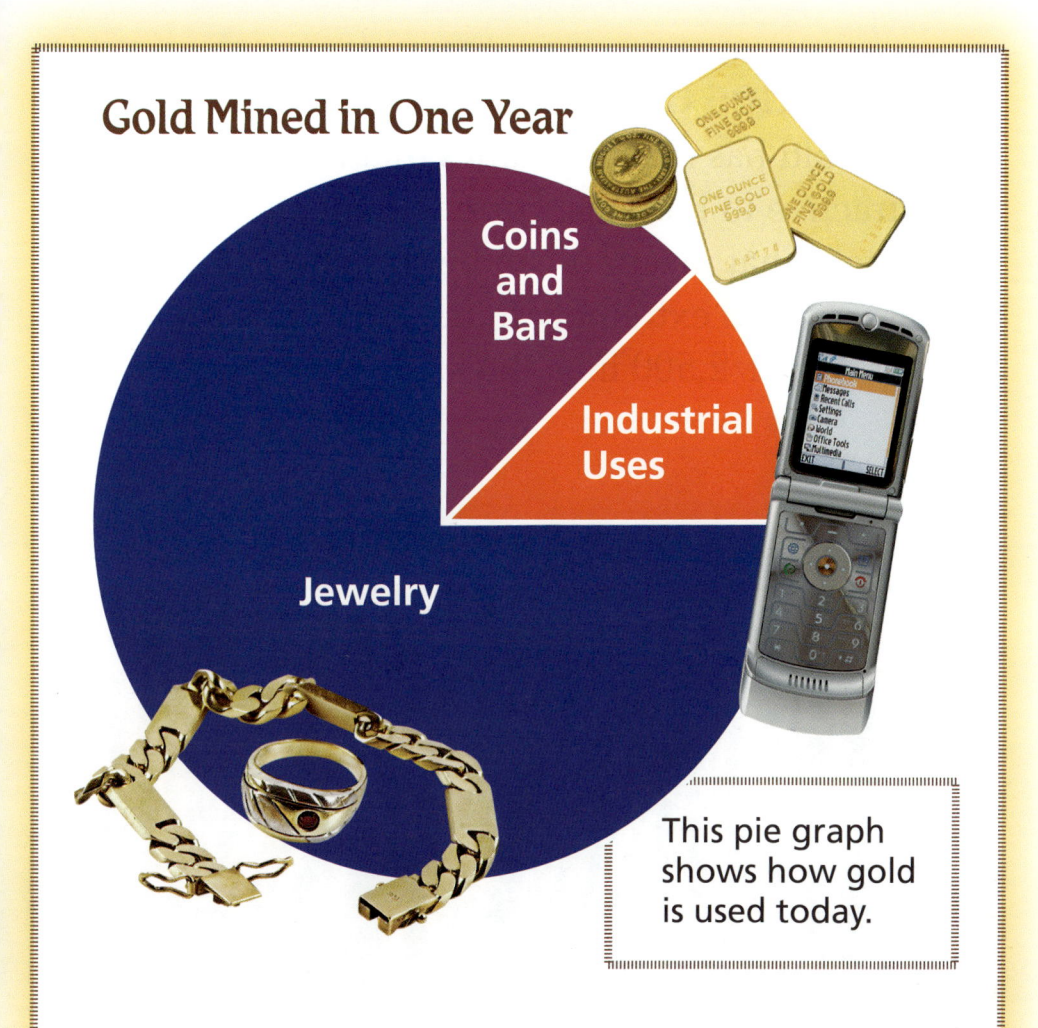

This pie graph shows how gold is used today.

Gold is usually mined, or dug, from the ground. Gold is very rare and hard to find. In the past when someone found gold, people hurried there to find more. It was called a "gold rush."

Today most of the gold mined each year is made into jewelry. People also use it in gold coins and bars, and in phones, computers, TVs, and other electronics.

Qualities of Gold

Gold has many qualities that make it attractive to humans. For one thing, it is a soft metal. That means it can be stretched into wire or pounded extremely thin. Gold wires can be less than 1/2,500 inch thick.

Long ago, gold was important in artwork. In some places, it was used as money.

Gold conducts electricity. This means electricity can flow through it.

Gold is very durable and reliable, which means it lasts and lasts. It doesn't tarnish or change. It stays clean and shiny for hundreds of years.

Gold in Electronics

Let's say you received an important phone call. You wouldn't be happy if you lost your call in the middle. Gold is used in phones to make sure those important calls stay connected.

Most phones include 30 or more contact points made of gold. If the contact points were made of another metal, they might tarnish, and the electrical current would be easily broken.

About one billion cell phones are made each year. About 50 cents worth of gold is in each. That's about $500,000,000 of gold used in phones each year! Gold keeps the electrical current in phones flowing smoothly for many years.

Gold is used in many places in a computer to make sure the computer works smoothly. Information flows through a computer from one part to another. The connectors on most of the parts that carry this information are covered with gold.

Gold is also used in televisions, calculators, GPS (global positioning system) units, stereos, and other electronics.

Although only a small amount of gold is used in one cell phone, television, or calculator, it really adds up in all these electronics. People can recycle resources such as gold from old electronics.

Your old electronics can be recycled.

Gold Keeps Out Heat

Gold shines because it reflects light so well. That's why scientists use a film of gold in the cockpit windows of airplanes. The film protects pilots from the heat and blinding light of the sun. A film of gold also is used in the windows of many new skyscrapers to keep out the glare and heat. This saves energy.

A film of gold on an astronaut's visor reflects the sun, but lets him or her see.

Gold also protects astronauts, satellites, and space equipment from the sun. A film of gold that is 6 millionths of an inch thick is enough to reflect sunlight.

Gold Keeps Us Safe

What helps the air bags inflate in a car crash?
GOLD!

What metal is used in an airplane's controls to keep it flying safely?
GOLD!

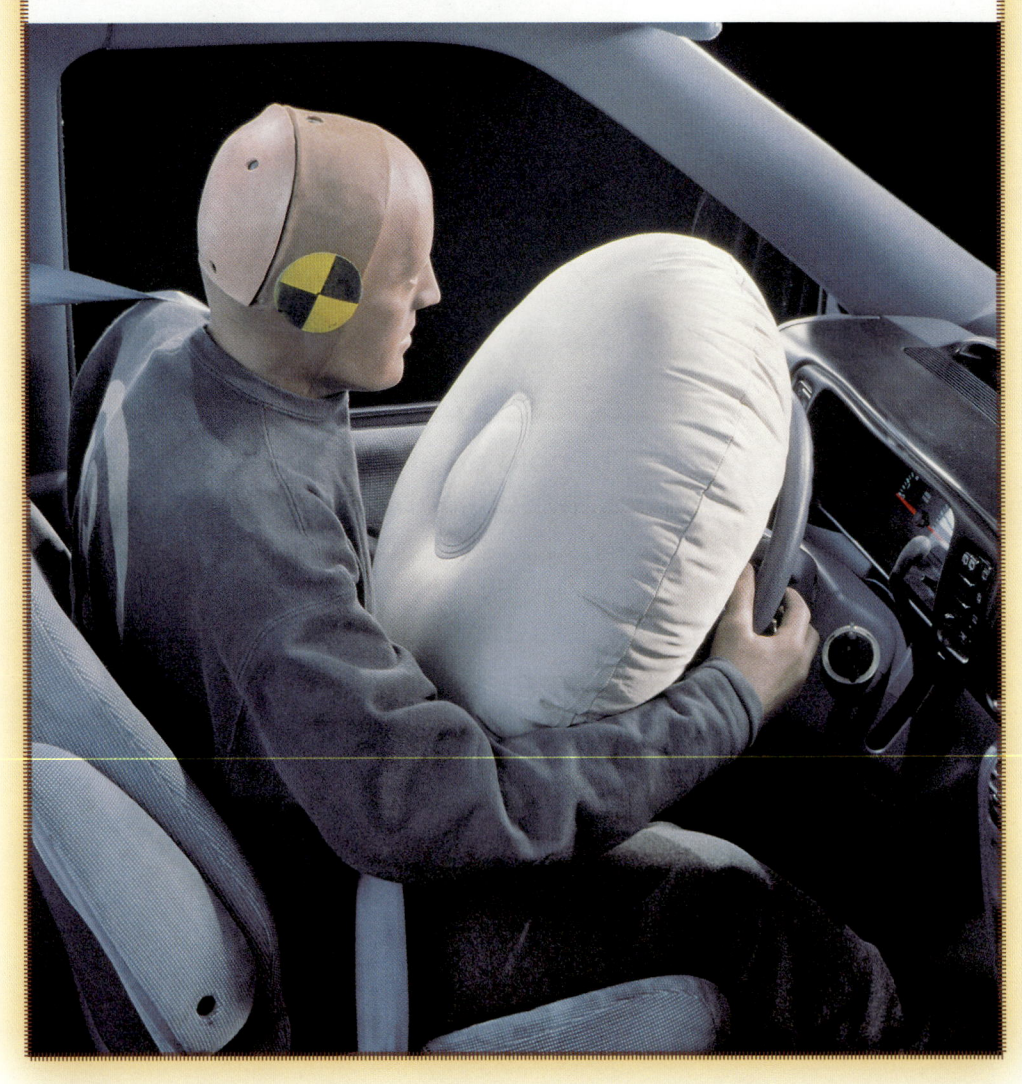

A firefighter's visor has tiny amounts of gold in it.

What reflects heat and light during a fire?
GOLD!

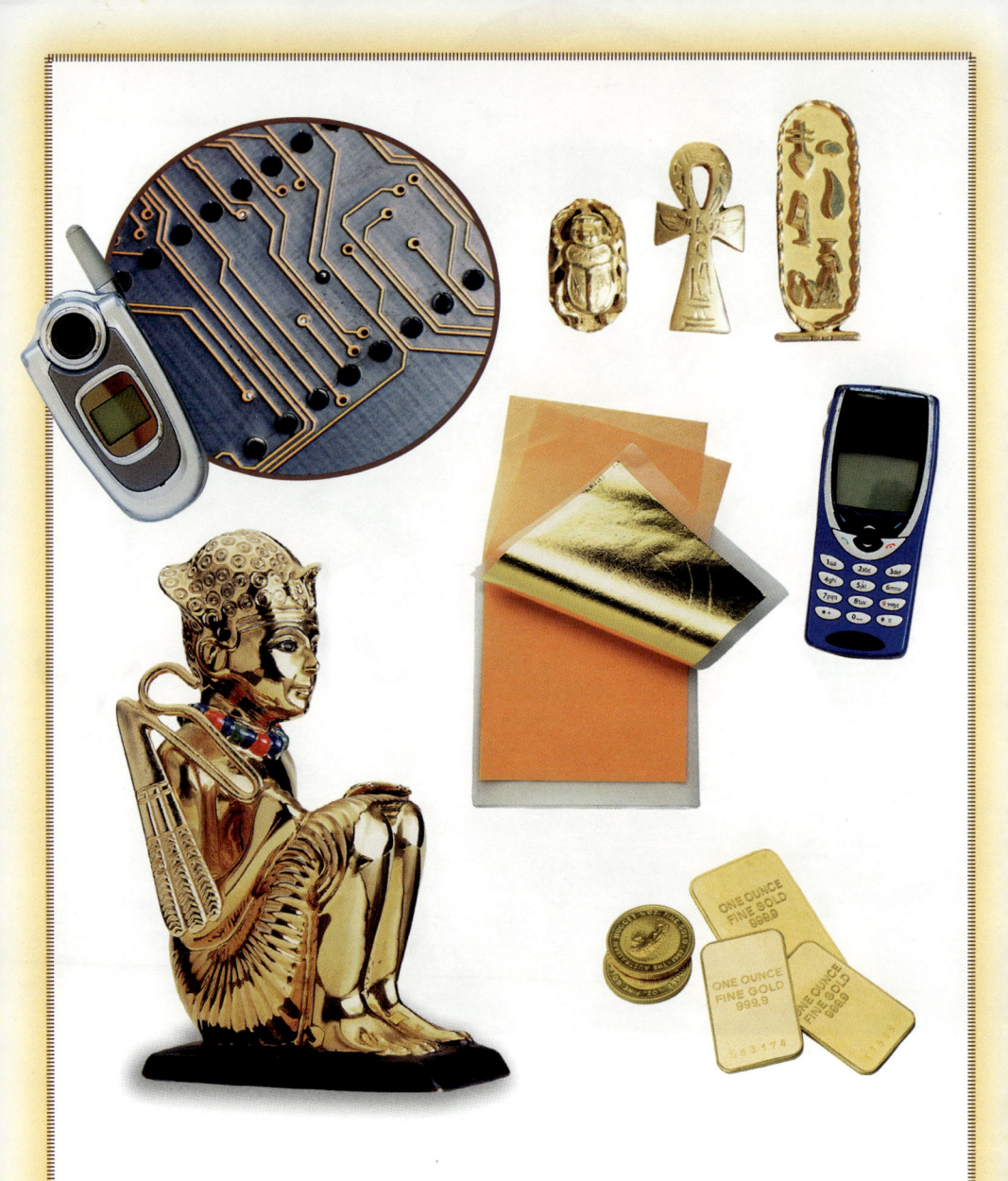

The many qualities of gold help keep us safe and keep modern electronics working well.

It's no wonder people say that things are AS GOOD AS **GOLD!**